HOW DO I BECOME A . . . ?

FIREFIGHTER

Mindi Rose Englart

Photographs by Peter Casolino

BLACKBIRCH®
PRESS

THOMSON

GALE

San Diego • Detroit • New York • San Francisco • Cleveland • New Haven, Conn. • Waterville, Maine • London • Munich

For more information, contact
The Gale Group, Inc.
27500 Drake Rd.
Farmington Hills, MI 48331-3535
Or you can visit our Internet site at http://www.gale.com

Photo Credits: Cover, all photos © Peter Casolino

LIBRARY OF CONGRESS CATALOGING-IN-PUBLICATION DATA

Englart, Mindi.
  Firefighter / by Mindi Rose Englart.
    p. cm. — (How do I become a: series)
Includes index.
Summary: Describes the work of a firefighter, including various duties, education and training needed, and equipment used.
  ISBN 1-56711-687-6 (hardcover)
  1. Fire extinction—Vocational guidance—Juvenile literature. 2.
Firefighters—Juvenile literature. [1. Firefighters. 2. Fire extinction—
Vocational guidance. 3. Vocational guidance.] I. Title. II. Series.
  TH9119 .E53 2003
  363.37'023—dc21   2002007249

Printed in China
10 9 8 7 6 5 4 3 2

CONTENTS

Dedication
To people who risk their lives to help others, and to my best friend Laura Sonnentag.

Special Thanks
The publisher and the author would like to thank New Haven's Fire Chief Dennis Daniels, Battalion Chief Paul Sandella, Lieutenant Karl Luschenat, and the firefighters at the Whitney Avenue and Goffe Street fire stations for their generous help in putting this book together. We would also like to thank the leaders and students at the Connecticut Fire Academy.

Every American community has a team of firefighters that puts out fires. Firefighters protect lives and property. Some firefighters make a career of this work. Others volunteer at local fire departments. All the brave men and women who choose to be firefighters are dedicated to helping others. Firefighting is difficult and dangerous work. A firefighter must be well trained to work safely. How do firefighters learn to fight fires?

Firefighters do difficult and dangerous work. ▶

So You Want to Be a Firefighter

Many kids want to be firefighters when they grow up. That is probably because it is an exciting and rewarding job!

Firefighters do more than fight fires. They rescue people who have been in car accidents. They respond to fire alarms and forest fires. Firefighters help during floods and brushfires. They are called when people smell gas, and when electrical wires are down. They are called when people get stuck in elevators. And they even rescue pets once in a while!

FIREFIGHTER

Though being a firefighter is a rewarding job, it can also be dangerous. About 100 firefighters die each year in the United States—and about 100,000 are injured.

▲ All kinds of emergencies require the help of firefighters.

It is not easy to get a job as a firefighter. Sometimes, thousands of people apply for one firefighting job! People who want to be firefighters must pass a special written test called a civil service test. After they pass this written test, they have a medical exam. Then, they take a test to make sure they are physically fit. They do weightlifting, sit-ups, and a 1.5 mile run. Those who pass these tests are interviewed by a group of people—including the fire chief. Those who are chosen go to a fire academy to train.

◄ Firefighters must be ready to respond to an emergency at any time.

Fire Academy

People need special training to become firefighters. They must attend a fire academy. At a fire academy, students, called recruits, learn what to do during emergencies. All recruits learn special firefighting skills. They are taught how to use fire hoses and hydrants. They learn how to put out fires, and how to maintain fire equipment.

The Connecticut Fire Academy is located in Windsor Locks, Connecticut. ▼

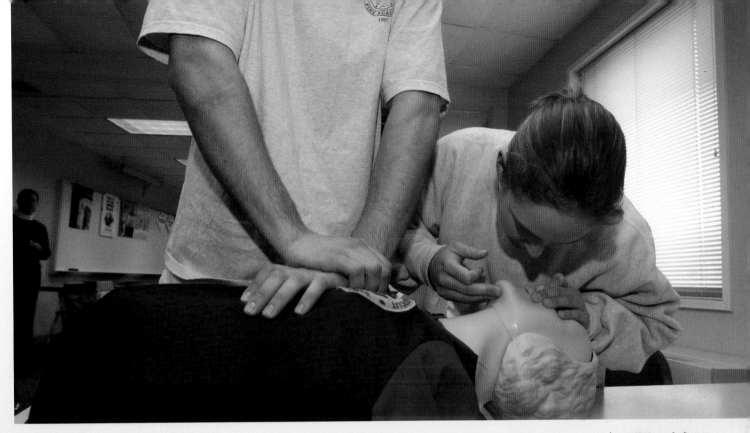

At the Connecticut Fire Academy in Windsor Locks, Connecticut, one special kind of training is hazardous materials (hazmat) training. Recruits are trained to help clean up oil spills. They also learn how to clean up other poisonous materials. They learn to use special vacuum cleaners and other equipment for this work. They are taught how to get people out of affected areas safely. This can be dangerous work. Recruits also get Emergency Medical Training (EMT). This training gives firefighters basic lifesaving skills.

Firefighting Equipment

Recruits must learn to use fire equipment properly. Two of the most important pieces of equipment are the fire truck and the fire engine. People often confuse fire trucks with fire engines, but they are different. A fire truck has ladders, and a fire engine has a pump.

◄ **Ladders are a very important part of a fire truck.**

▲ **A fire truck has lots of ladders.**

Fire Trucks

A fire truck (also called a ladder truck) has lots of ladders. They range from 14 to 50 feet long. The smallest one is called a dinky ladder. It's a small, foldable ladder that allows firefighters to reach attics and other narrow places. Recruits practice ladder training on these small ladders at first. They slowly build up their balance and strength. Eventually, they are able to climb tall ladders that can reach 4 to 5 stories high.

▲ Fire engines can carry 500 gallons of water.

Fire Engines

Fire engines carry and pump water. They can carry up to 500 gallons of water. That is enough water to spray for a few minutes. Then, hoses must be hooked up to a hydrant. A hydrant provides a much larger supply of water.

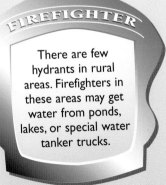

FIREFIGHTER

There are few hydrants in rural areas. Firefighters in these areas may get water from ponds, lakes, or special water tanker trucks.

Water hoses must be kept clean and ready for use. ▶

The most important part of a fire engine is its pump. Pumps create energy that forces water out of hoses very quickly. Water pours out of fire hydrants at about 50 pounds per minute. After water is pushed through the pump, though, it comes out at 150 pounds per minute! Firefighters need this powerful flow of water to help put fires out fast.

Sometimes one firefighter uses a deck gun at the top of the engine. A deck gun is a powerful water tool. It can direct water at a rate of up to 1,000 gallons per minute.

Hoses are stored at the back of a fire engine. Hoses are made of nylon. They are covered with thick canvas to make them strong. Hoses can be linked together to reach fires that are far away from the engine.

Other Fire Vehicles

Some departments have special fire vehicles. For example, the aerial tower, or aerial platform, truck has guns that can shoot up to 1,000 gallons of water per minute. It doesn't have a pump, so it needs to be connected to a fire engine. The aerial tower truck has equipment that lifts firefighters up to high places.

Firefighters sometimes use a tiller truck. A firefighter uses a second steering wheel at the back of this truck. Tiller trucks can make difficult turns. They are able to get into hard-to-reach areas.

◀ **An aerial tower has guns that can shoot up to 1,000 gallons of water per minute.**

Putting Out a Practice Fire

After recruits have learned to use firefighting equipment, they practice battling real fires. The Connecticut Fire Academy has buildings, cars, and even a mock airplane to set on fire. This practice helps recruits learn what it will be like to fight fires.

Practice fires are called drills. During a drill, an instructor acts as a lieutenant, a captain, or a battalion chief. His or her job is to supervise the recruits. One recruit connects the hose from the engine to a fire hydrant. Another recruit holds the hose and points it at the fire. The hose is difficult to manage when water rushes through it. Recruits learn how to hold the hose steady and to aim it directly at the fire. They learn how to use the controls that adjust the flow of water from the hose. All recruits learn to concentrate and to work fast.

Each recruit has a job to do ▼
during a drill.

Physical Training

Firefighting is hard work. Firefighters wear gear and carry tools that can weigh more than 45 pounds. The weight they carry can increase to 100 pounds if they carry a hose or if they get wet.

Firefighters need to be in good shape to do their jobs. Recruits exercise as part of their training. This helps them to build up their strength. They wear their gear and carry heavy equipment when they run up stairs during a fire. They work in all kinds of weather conditions. Sometimes they must climb up to high places or crawl through smoky buildings.

Recruits exercise by running up and down the steps of a building. ▶

The Gear

Firefighters wear special gear to keep them safe. An important piece of their gear is an air tank. Air tanks allow firefighters to breathe for about 30 minutes in heavy smoke. Firefighters use more air when they run up stairs carrying heavy equipment. Under these conditions, the air in the tank might only last 15 minutes. Firefighters learn to adjust the flow of air so they can breathe while they work.

◀ **Air tanks allow firefighters to breathe in smoky conditions.**

New Haven firefighters pose ▲
in the special gear they use.

Firefighters wear special jackets and pants that do not easily catch fire. There is reflective tape on their pants and jackets. When light shines on the tape, firefighters can see each other. They wear helmets and masks to protect their heads and faces. They carry rescue ropes to lower themselves from burning buildings. They may also carry a knife, a flashlight, gloves, and other tools. Most firefighters carry a wedge to prop open doors. They carry a two-way radio, a notepad, and a pen to do reports.

Helmets and masks protect ▶
firefighters' heads and faces.

▲ **Special tools help firefighters break down doors and walls.**

Other Firefighting Tools

Firefighters carry special tools to help them to get into buildings and vehicles quickly. These tools are used to break open steel doors. Firefighters can also use them to break down walls to rescue people from a burning building.

The fire chief may have a special camera that shows areas of heat in lighter shades than other areas. This helps firefighters find a hidden fire quickly.

Many fire departments use a book that has maps of every street in a town or city. The quickest way from the firehouse to each street is marked. This makes it easy for a fire department to find the location of a fire.

At the Firehouse

After academy training, firefighters are assigned to firehouses. They are a lot like other houses. There are beds, a kitchen, and showers in most firehouses. There may be a television or gym equipment in the building. Between alarms, firefighters do chores. They clean up, make their beds, and take out the garbage—just as people do in their homes.

Sometimes hours go by between fire alarms. Firefighters rest, exercise, and train on fire equipment. They often cook and eat meals together. This time together helps them to work better as a team.

▼ **A firefighter cooks breakfast for his firehouse.**

The watch booth is where a firefighter sits to take calls. If there is an emergency, he or she will sound an alarm.

Firefighters must be ready to go out on calls at all times. There is always a firefighter stationed at the watch booth. This is an office where a firefighter sits to take phone calls and to greet visitors. When there is a call, the firefighter in the watch booth sounds an alarm. This lets the other firefighters know that there is an emergency.

To save time, firefighters sometimes slide down a fire pole instead of using the stairs. A fire pole can be up to 30 feet tall. Some fire departments don't have fire poles, because they can cause injuries.

Checks and Testing

Firefighters work for lengths of time called shifts. A new crew of firefighters comes on duty each morning. They have a short meeting with the group that was on duty the night before. Then they begin their equipment checks. It's important to make sure that everything works at each shift change—there won't be time if the alarm sounds.

▼ Equipment is checked at each shift change to be sure that everything works.

It is important to check that the nozzle on the fire hose is clean.

Each morning someone tests the fire alarm to make sure it works. Then, firefighters begin their list of daily chores. For example, drivers change the battery in the two-way radio. They check the trucks to be sure that the lights and sirens work. This is called the pre-trip check. They also check the trucks' brakes and controls.

Firefighters check their air tanks to make sure they are full of oxygen. They check their medical equipment and supplies. They also check their medical bags—which hold oxygen, scissors, and ice packs. Medical bags also contain water, Band-Aids, bandages, and kits for delivering babies.

September 11, 2001

On September 11, 2001, many people were killed when terrorists flew airplanes into the World Trade Center and the Pentagon. Americans watched film footage that showed the bravery of firefighters, police officers, and other emergency workers.

New York City firefighters ran into the World Trade Center even as other people ran out. Their mission was to save lives. Many of them died. The firefighters who worked that day showed the nation the heroic work firefighters perform every day.

▲ **New York City firefighters showed the world how brave firefighters are when they attempted to rescue people trapped in the World Trade Center.**

A Call for Help

Calls to 911 are directed to local police and/or fire departments. If a call is a fire or rescue emergency, the information is sent to the fire department. The person in the watch booth turns on the lights and alarm in the firehouse. Firefighters rush to find out what the emergency is. If they are upstairs, they may use the fire pole to get downstairs quickly. Firefighters hurry to get into their gear and to drive to the scene.

◄ **A firefighter must get into his or her gear quickly and rush to the scene of an emergency.**

At the Scene

When there is an emergency, the fire chief is in charge of the scene—even over other emergency workers and the police. Firefighters often need to make a scene safe for others to enter. A fire chief has a lot of responsibility. He or she needs to make life-and-death decisions quickly. For example, a chief decides whether to call for more fire trucks and engines.

When a fire alarm sounds, there is no time to decide who will do what. Firefighters must know what to do. They must take their places immediately. Firefighters who use fire engines must get right to work.

During a fire, firefighters ▶
make the site safe for other
emergency workers.

25

◀ **New Haven fire chief,
Chief Daniels.**

Firefighting is all about teamwork. One person cannot put out a big fire alone. The team that works with the fire engine usually has a driver, a hydrant person, a pipe person, and an officer. Each person has a job to do during a fire. The hydrant person attaches the hose to a fire hydrant. The driver adjusts gauges to create a strong, steady stream of water through the hose. The pipe person uses the hose to put water on the fire. The officer supervises the others.

The chief looks at the scene to determine if lives are in danger. If so, he or she orders firefighters to rescue those who are trapped. If the chief sees that hazardous materials have been spilled, he or she will call on the hazmat team to clean it up.

◀ **The hose person lays the hose
out so the water can flow freely.**

Letting smoke out of a burning building is very important. Smoke causes more fire-related deaths than burns.

Ladder Work

Ladder company firefighters get ladders to the fire. Firefighters use ladders to climb up sides of buildings to rescue people. They also use ladders to get high enough to break windows. They can get high enough to saw into roofs to make holes that let smoke out. They must get smoke out of the building so the people inside can breathe.

Firefighters use ladders to get high enough to saw holes in a roof. This lets smoke out so people inside can breathe. ▶

Escape Tools

Firefighters are sometimes called to help in emergencies other than fires. People who have been in car accidents can be stuck in wrecked cars. Firefighters may be called to help victims get out.

Firefighters have tools to help people who are stuck in something and cannot get out. More than one tool is often used at once. One of these tools, called a cutter, can cut through most metal. Cutters can take the roof off of a car!

Firefighters also use spreaders. With this tool, they can open a very small space—such as a closed car door—up to 32 inches. Another tool is used to push dashboards away from people who are stuck in a car after an accident.

◄ **Firefighters use special tools to cut metal, to push back dashboads, and to pry open jammed car doors.**

Firefighters also use special airbags. These airbags are powerful enough to lift a truck. In fact, the biggest airbag can lift 734 tons! Firefighters put wood blocks under a large vehicle's tires so that it can't roll.

▼ Special air bags can lift up to 734 tons. Firefighters use these to lift vehicles.

Search and Rescue

Firefighters work in pairs to find and remove trapped victims. This is called search and rescue. It is difficult to see inside a dark, smoky building. It is also hard to hear over the roar of flames. Firefighters must remain calm and think clearly. They may use a hose as a line to follow to get out of a smoky building. Firefighters carefully move people with injuries to a safe area. If necessary, they perform first aid on victims.

During search and rescue emergencies, firefighters must remain calm and work together. ▼

A Job Well Done

Firefighters need to rest and recover after some emergencies. They may need oxygen to help them breathe after they've been in heavy smoke. Sometimes their eyes are red and sore from the smoke. Firefighters and rescue workers help each other when they are injured. Then it's back to the firehouse to wait for the next call!

After most emergencies, firefighters are tired, dirty, and need to rest. ▶

Glossary

Air tank   Container of compressed air that helps firefighters breathe in smoky situations

Fire engine   A vehicle that carries and pumps water

Fire truck   A vehicle that carries ladders

Hazmat   Poisonous materials

Hydrant   A pipe used by firefighters that is connected to a main water source

Recruit   Student who studies at a fire academy

For More Information

United States Fire Administration

www.usfa.fema.gov/kids

This website has games and information about fire safety.

Index